W9-CQD-306

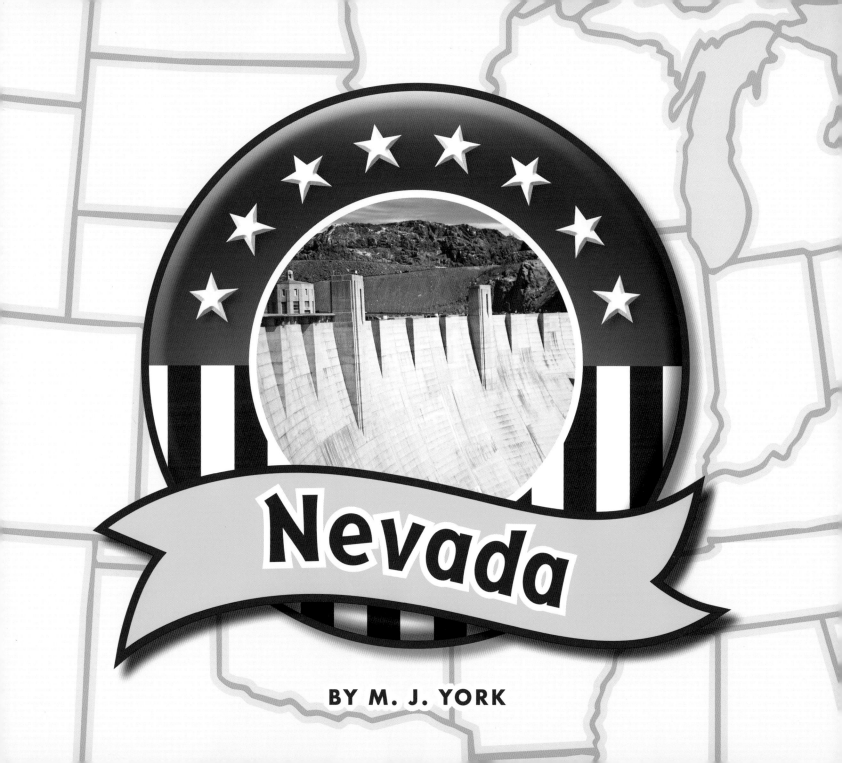

Nevada

BY M. J. YORK

The Child's World

Published by The Child's World®
1980 Lookout Drive • Mankato, MN 56003-1705
800-599-READ • www.childsworld.com

ACKNOWLEDGMENTS
The Child's World®: Mary Berendes, Publishing Director
The Design Lab: Design and production
Red Line Editorial: Editorial direction

PHOTO CREDITS: Big Stock Photo, cover, 1, 3; Matt Kania/Map Hero,
Inc., 4, 5; Shutterstock Images, 7; Chee-Onn Leong/Shutterstock Images, 9;
iStockphoto, 10; Bob Reynolds/Shutterstock Images, 11; Charles A Blakeslee/
Photolibrary, 13; Photolibrary, 15; Matthew Jones/iStockphoto, 17; Vincent
Yu/AP Images, 19; Celso Diniz/Shutterstock Images, 21; One Mile Up, 22;
Quarter-dollar coin image from the United States Mint, 22

LIBRARY OF CONGRESS CATALOGING-IN-PUBLICATION DATA
York, M. J., 1983-
  Nevada / by M.J. York.
    p. cm.
  Includes bibliographical references and index.
  ISBN 978-1-60253-472-8 (library bound : alk. paper)
  1. Nevada—Juvenile literature. I. Title.

F841.3.Y67 2010
979.3—dc22

2010017930

Printed in the United States of America in Mankato, Minnesota.
July 2010
F11538

On the cover:
The Hoover Dam
is on the border
between Nevada
and Arizona.

CONTENTS

4 Geography

6 Cities

8 Land

10 Plants and Animals

12 People and Work

14 History

16 Ways of Life

18 Famous People

20 Famous Places

22 *State Symbols*

23 *Glossary*

24 *Further Information*

24 *Index*

Geography

Let's explore Nevada! Nevada is in the southwestern United States.

OREGON

IDAHO

WYOMING

•Gerlach

•Elko

NEVADA

Reno
•

•Virginia City

Lake
Tahoe

★ **Carson City**

•Austin

•Eureka

•Ely

UTAH

•Tonopah

•Caliente

CALIFORNIA

Las Vegas
•

Henderson•

Boulder City

Hoover Dam

Colorado River

NORTH

WEST   EAST

SOUTH

*Pacific
Ocean*

ARIZONA

Cities

Carson City is the capital of Nevada.

Las Vegas is the largest city in the state.

Many **tourists** come to Las Vegas each year.

Reno and Henderson are other large cities.

Las Vegas has many hotels and restaurants. ▶

Land

Nevada is dry. The land is mostly desert. However, the Colorado River is in the southeastern part of the state. Nevada has many mountains.

The word Nevada means "snow-capped" in Spanish. This refers to the state's mountains.

Red Rock Canyon is a desert area west of Las Vegas. ▶

Plants and Animals

Nevada's plants and animals must be able to live in the dry heat. Nevada's state animal is the desert bighorn sheep. It needs little water to drink. The state **reptile** is the desert tortoise. It can live for 70 years. The state bird is the mountain bluebird.

Desert bighorn sheep live in the mountains of Nevada. ▶

People and Work

Nevada is home to more than 2.6 million people. Many people work in jobs that serve people who visit the state. These include jobs in hotels or **casinos**. Mining is an important **industry** in Nevada.

Nevada is known as "the Silver State" because of its silver mines.

Silver, gold, and other minerals have been mined in Nevada for many years. ▶

History

Native Americans have lived in the Nevada area for thousands of years. White settlers came to the area in the 1850s. They discovered gold in 1859. Nevada became the thirty-sixth state on October 31, 1864. Around this time, many Native Americans were moved to **reservations**. In 1931, Nevada made **gambling** legal. This led to more tourists visiting the state.

In the 1870s, Silver City, Nevada, was a silver-mining town. ▶

15

Ways of Life

Las Vegas has many things to do. People see shows and gamble. They stay in big hotels and go shopping. People also enjoy Nevada's natural beauty. They **hike** and camp in the mountains and the deserts.

Las Vegas's hotels and casinos bring many visitors each year. ▶

Famous People

Tennis star Andre Agassi was born in Nevada. Many **entertainers** live in Las Vegas, including singer Wayne Newton and animal trainers Siegfried and Roy.

Andre Agassi won many important tennis ▶ tournaments during his career.

Famous Places

The Hoover **Dam** is on the Colorado River in Nevada. It is one of the largest dams in the world. Lake Tahoe is a **popular** place for fun in the water. People also ski there during the winter.

The Hoover Dam is made of concrete and is 726 feet (221 m) tall. ▶

State Symbols

Seal

Nevada's seal has pictures that stand for Nevada's industry, history, and natural features. The seal also has the state **motto**, "All for our Country." Go to childsworld.com/links for a link to Nevada's state Web site, where you can get a firsthand look at the state seal.

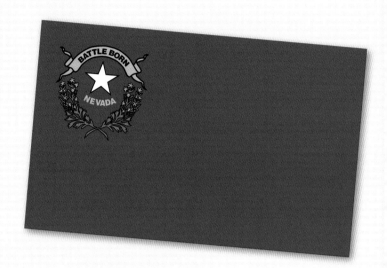

Flag

Nevada's state flag has the sagebrush, the state flower.

Quarter

Nevada's state quarter shows wild horses and mountains. The quarter came out in 2006.

Glossary

casinos (kuh-SEE-noze): Casinos are places where people go to gamble. Some people in Nevada work in casinos.

dam (DAM): A dam is a structure that is built across a river or a lake to hold back the water. The Hoover Dam is in Nevada.

entertainers (en-tur-TAYN-urz): Entertainers are people who make others laugh or enjoy something. Some famous entertainers live and work in Las Vegas.

gambling (GAM-bling): Gambling is betting money on games or things that happen by chance. Gambling is popular in Las Vegas.

hike (HYK): To hike is to take a walk in a natural area, such as a hill or a mountain. Some people come to Nevada to hike.

industry (IN-duh-stree): An industry is a type of business or trade. Silver mining is an important industry in Nevada.

motto (MOT-oh): A motto is a sentence that states what people stand for or believe. Nevada's motto is "All for our Country."

popular (POP-yuh-lur): To be popular is to be enjoyed by many people. Lake Tahoe is a popular place to visit.

reptile (REP-tyl): A reptile is a cold-blooded animal that crawls or slithers near the ground. Nevada's state reptile is the desert tortoise.

reservations (rez-ur-VAY-shunz): Reservations are areas of land that are saved for a certain use. Many Native Americans in Nevada were moved to reservations.

seal (SEEL): A seal is a symbol a state uses for government business. Nevada's seal has the state motto.

symbols (SIM-bulz): Symbols are pictures or things that stand for something else. Nevada's state flag shows symbols for the state's industry and history.

tourists (TOOR-ists): Tourists are people who visit a place (such as a state or country) for fun. Many tourists come to Nevada.

Further Information

Books

Coerr, Eleanor. *S is for Silver: A Nevada Alphabet*. Chelsea, MI: Sleeping Bear Press, 2004.

Keller, Laurie. *The Scrambled States of America*. New York: Henry Holt, 2002.

Labella, Susan. *Nevada*. New York: Children's Press, 2007.

Web Sites

Visit our Web site for links about Nevada: *childsworld.com/links*

Note to Parents, Teachers, and Librarians: We routinely verify our Web links to make sure they are safe and active sites. So encourage your readers to check them out!

Index

activities, 16, 20
capital, 6
Colorado River, 8, 20
Hoover Dam, 20
jobs, 12

Lake Tahoe, 20
Las Vegas, 6, 16, 18
Native Americans, 14
population, 12

settlers, 14
state animal, 10
state bird, 10
state reptile, 10
tourism, 6, 12, 14, 16